Introduction

Hi! If you're reading this, you're in the same position I was in just a short while ago. I promise you, with the right oomf you can do just about anything. Before you know it, it'll all be over, believe me. Getting into vet school is a challenge, in the recent years, hundreds and thousands of applicants have fought over the sacred places that the eight schools have to offer. And if all goes well, you lucky people will be getting the chance to attend the brand new ninth vet school that's to come - it seems pretty awesome.

I've written this book for UK school leavers who want to go to a UK vet school like I did. It's the only way I have experienced getting into vet school, so it's the only way I know how.

Look, I'll try and condense the information I have as much as I can, but, if I'm going to try and help you out, I have to do it right. By just reading this book, it shows yourself how committed you are to the vet career, but, that's no guarantee you will get a precious place. You *must* have the drive for it. Your interviewers have to see that *you* want it more than anyone else. From my oh so rough calculations, there's maybe a thousand places up for grabs each year for UK applicants, that is, when all the vet schools are combined. That's not so many when you consider the number of people getting into let's say a psychology course. There are around 50 universities who teach psychology, each have on average 100-200 spaces, that's a lot of damn spaces. I envied my friends who applied to such courses, I even considered dropping my dream and take an easier route. But I persevered. The split second you get that UCAS acceptance to any vet school, it all seems worth it.

Hey, if I can do it, anyone can do it. I was the girl who teachers told to speak up in class, the one who had to have their parents ask the teacher not to make me read out loud to the class. I was shy, a quality I thought no vet student could have. A few years before my application, I squirmed at the thought of sitting in front of an interview, I questioned if I did graduate vet school, would I be able to talk to clients, or would I shy away? So you know what I did? I pushed myself to the limit.

Get your pencils ready, we're in for a ride, because just like the veterinary application process, you have to do a lot of it yourself.

Passion

Passion, how cheesy. But when you pursue a career like this, it's vital that you're pumped with it. You have to really consider the vet dream, it will hit you like a bus if you're not totally in for it. Okay, I told you to have your pencils ready. Now, below, complete the bullet points, explain to me why you're passionate about being a vet. And I don't want any cute short answers like "I Love Animals." I want solid reasons, that you could say to an interviewer without sounding like a lost child.

-

-

You done? I don't think so, I think you could dig a little deeper. Go on. Once you've done that I'll shut up and you can take a little biscuit break if you please.

Grades

Your grades. They matter if you like it or not. Vet schools will cut you off the second you miss a single grade. Some of them don't even allow you to amend them by resitting. It's a brutal game. But why do they do it? It's an easy way to dry up the applicant pool, of course. The subjects also matter, each vet school has slightly different requirements but you should be able to put them all in one basket by taking the highest approved courses in the field. Chemistry, Biology, and Maths. I actually broke this rule, instead of maths, I took physics. It was more practical in my eyes, I enjoyed it. From physics I can explain how stars arise, how electrons can be waves *and* particles in the same instant. Maths never interested me, also, I think the vet schools liked my change in scenery.

I'm Scottish, by the way. There's no difference in how I got into vet school than anyone in one of the other three countries of the UK apart from the qualifications at school I received. I'm pretty well versed in A-Levels, AS and GCSEs but I took National 5s (a bit tougher than GCSEs but we only have to do 6), Highers (these were our important ones, a little easier than AS, we had to do a minimum of 5) and Advanced Highers (basically A-Levels but tougher - BB at advanced higher is seen to be equivalent to AAA at A-Level). I have to say, I got straight As, but that's what you need to stand out (no, we don't have A*s). I'm sorry, everyone from Wales and Northern Ireland, but us wee countries don't get as much recognition as England. I've got to say, I didn't even know you guys did A-Levels as well until I researched it for this book.

Back to the grades, basically do the very best you can, and then a bit better. I'll condense all of the grade requirements later on so you don't have to flick through each university's website like I had to. See? I can be nice.

Work Experience

Get. As. Much. Work. Experience. As. You. Possibly. Can.

The vet schools love work experience, most of them even require it. The reasons to do it are: firstly, you can prove to yourself that you're cut out for being a vet. Secondly, you *must* also prove that to the universities. Thirdly, you'll be able to make connections early on in your career. And fourthly, you'll probably enjoy it, I did. Living in the city, I didn't get many chances to work on huge farms, but when I did, it was bloody amazing. Now, if you're applying to vet school in the near future (within a year or two), I want you to get your pencil out again. Do it. You got one? Great. Please go ahead and tick off every type of work experience you have done on the next page. In an ideal world, it would be all of them, but everyone has different opportunities in life. I know for certain I could've only ticked six of these things off the list when I applied.

Type of Work Experience	Tick if completed
A week at a Small Animal Vet Practice (preferably 2)	
A week at a Large Animal Vet Practice	
A week on a Dairy Farm	
A week Lambing	
A week with Exotics	
A week at a Mixed Farm	
A half day at an Abattoir	
A week at a Stables	
A week at a cattery or dog kennel (preferable both)	
A week at a 'strange' Animal Farm (for example, Alpacas)	

This list is what people normally say is a base line, within each section many believe you should have multiple weeks. Don't worry about these people, while it would certainly boost your application, and make the interviews a little easier, the amount of stress that some people feel when they think they don't have enough weeks of work experience breaks my heart. I'm going to be honest, I only had 9 weeks and 1 day of work experience under my belt, I've met people who have over 50 weeks. I'm proof that you don't need to go over the top and don't have to spend every waking day you're off school shovelling crap in a freezing field.

You're allowed some time off, especially during exam season. Never let getting that extra week of work experience let you miss out on a grade. The vet schools don't care about your twenty-third week, if you miss a grade, even by one letter, you'll be forgotten. That's the hard truth of it all.

Now, diaries. You should definitely have a diary or a notebook, or something to write down everything you've done on your work experience. I made the mistake of thinking I'd remember everything very early on, only to find that a year later I had no idea what I'd done for the entire week at the stables apart from cleaning up paddocks and stuffing hay into bags. When you have to prepare for your interviews, you have to know the minor details, but I'll get to that later. REMEMBER - get references from the places you work at, many universities require them at interview stage - you don't want to be like me and scramble for them the week before your interview.

The Vet Schools

So, you've got the grades, you've got the work experience, now all you have to do is apply (usually by the 15th of October), it sounds so simple. I've been kind enough to put a checklist by each university to ensure you don't miss anything during or after your application. I'll list the universities in alphabetical order, there's no favouritism from me here guys.

The university you apply to is very important, they all teach in different ways, they all look for different things in applicants, they all have different application processes, it's tough. I recommend you go to the open days at the universities you plan to apply to so you definitely know it's right for you. You'll be there for five or six years, it's worth the day trip with your parents. Remember, you can only apply to four vet schools in one application cycle, so choose wisely.

Bristol - Five Years

This course is pretty interesting, you spend the first three years in the heart of Bristol with the students from all the other courses, but they go off and graduate and you still have two years left, so what do you do? The final two years of the course here are all at the main vet campus, so you just move out there. It's pretty cool. The buildings at the vet school are amazing, it really is beautiful. Even better, Bristol doesn't interview applicants, so if that's the part that scares you most about applying, Bristol would be the ideal place to apply. For every place available, Bristol gets 9 applicants.

Required Tasks	Tick when complete
Scottish Students: AAAA at Higher	
Scottish Students: AA at Advanced Higher, in Chemistry and either Biology, Physics or Maths	
Rest of UK Students: AAA at A level in Chemistry and two of Biology, Physics and Maths	
Fill out the Work Experience for and the Personal and Professional Attributes Form when it is sent to you by email - after your initial UCAS application	
Have at least one week of Veterinary Clinic Work Experience	
Have at least one week of Hands on Animal Husbandry	

Cambridge - Six Years

Good old Cambridge eh? If you love the theoretical side of veterinary medicine, this might be the course for you, although they have been raising the quality of their practical side recently. As we all know, Cambridge is gorgeous, it's known for its amazing buildings right? I guess it's probably better known for producing amazing academics. What's special about the course here is that you after two years of the veterinary course, you get a year off. Well, when I say a year off I mean you get to complete a one year intercalation year, you become a postgraduate half way through your course which is pretty cool. Then you continue on the vet course like nothing has happened. You get a thorough interview here though, so watch yourself. Work experience isn't required but still encouraged. For each place available at Cambridge, there are 4 people applying.

Required Tasks	Tick when complete
Scottish Students: AAA at Advanced Higher in Chemistry, Biology and Maths	
Rest of UK Students: "a few" A/A*s at GCSE	
Rest of UK Students: A*AA at A-Level in Chemistry, Biology and Maths	
Take the Natural Sciences Admissions Assessment after your initial UCAS application	
Interview - "Have a realistic idea of the vet career"	

Edinburgh - Five Years

Ah, nice and sunny Edinburgh - I'm only joking guys. I've got to say, even though they're seven miles from the centre of Edinburgh, the Vet Schools facilities never fail to amaze me. Edinburgh is accredited by countries all over the world. Their 'speciality' is exotics so if you love reptiles and birds, this might be the place for you. They use multiple mini interviews here (MMIs), it's basically seven 10 minute interviews back to back, so if you're not comfortable on a topic, you'll soon move on. Edinburgh yet again doesn't have any work experience *requirements* - but it's needed. There's a whole damn interview based off of work experience. Edinburgh's a tough school to get into, for each place they have on offer, there are 11 applicants.

Required Tasks	Tick when complete
Scottish Students: AAAAB at Higher, including an A in Chemistry and Biology, Physics is required at a pass at National 5	
Scottish Students: BB at Advanced Higher, including Chemistry and another science	
Rest of UK Students: AAA at A-Level in Chemistry, Biology and another subject	
Complete a Work Experience form soon after the initial UCAS application, it will be emailed to you	
Interview	

Glasgow - Five Years

The Glasgow vet school has its own catered accommodation on site, so you don't have to trudge far in the morning to get to your lectures. The scenic little campus is swarming with vet students. Glasgow is also accredited in countries from all over the globe, letting you take your career anywhere. Most first years live on campus, so your life is very vet orientated - which is great! The interview is a standard 'sit across the table from two people who ask you questions', you get two interviews, that are both 15 minutes each - it'll be over before you know it. There's also a computer based exercise that's half an hour long - to test your ethics. Glasgow, much like Edinburgh, have one space for every 11 applicants.

Required Tasks	Tick when complete
Scottish Students: AAAAB at Higher, to include Chemistry, Biology and either Maths or Physics	
Scottish Students: BB at Advanced Higher in Chemistry and Biology	
Rest of UK Students: AAA at A-Level in Chemistry, Biology and another subject (Careful! Art, Drama, PE, Music and Home ec. Don't count)	
Six weeks of Work Experience - Two of which should be in a Vet Clinic	
Interview	

Harper Adams - Keele - Five Years

I've got to be honest, this is a new vet school that no one knows the little details about but I'll do my best. From what a know, the two universities - Harper Adams and Keele - are combining, they have amazing agricultural facilities so I'm sure the vet school will be outstanding. Since it's a new school, they'll have all the latest equipment - which is exciting. The interviews are once again MMIs, that's about all I know. It is said that there will be 80 spaces available here each year, but since there hasn't been an application cycle for them, I don't know the space to applicant ratio.

Required Tasks	Tick when complete
Scottish Students: AABBB at Higher to include Chemistry and Biology	
Scottish Students: AA at Advanced Higher in either Chemistry and/or Biology	
Rest of UK Students: AAB but preferably AAA in two Sciences and another Subject	
Interview	
Two weeks of Work Experience in a Vet Clinic	
Four weeks of Hands on Animal Husbandry Work Experience	
Interview	

Liverpool - Five Years

Liverpool is set up is much like Bristols, you spend the first 3 years with everyone else in the city of Liverpool, and then move to the vet school for 2 years. Liverpool's 'speciality' is horses. The facilities are beautiful, and the semi-rural scenery around them is gorgeous. Liverpool has the MMIs, a series of six 5 minute stations, it really doesn't last long. For every space available, there are 6 applicants.

Required Tasks	Tick when compete
Scottish Students: AAAAB at Higher, including a A in Chemistry and Biology	
Scottish Students: BB at Advanced Higher in Chemistry and Biology	
Rest of UK Students: AAABBBB at GCSE including Maths, English, Physics	
Rest of UK Students: AAA at A-Level in Biology, Chemistry and another subject	
Two weeks of Vet Clinic Work Experience	
Three weeks of work experience in Animal Husbandry, you must have at least 4 days with at least two of: Cat/Dogs, Equine, or Farm Animals (ex. Dairy Farm)	
Fill out Work Experience questionnaire after initial UCAS application	
Interview	

Nottingham - Five Years

Known for being the highly practical, Vet Clinics see Nottingham graduates as the ones with the best day one competencies. The facilities are once again outstanding. There are three 20 minute parts to the interview, a sit down interview, a practical test, and a group activity. There's 1 place for every 6 applicants.

Required Tasks	Tick when complete
Scottish Students: AAAAA at National 5 to include Chemistry, Biology, either Physics or Maths, and English	
Scottish Students: AABBB at Higher in Biology and Chemistry	
Scottish Students: AA at Advanced Higher in Chemistry and Biology	
Rest of UK Students: AAAAA at GCSE in Chemistry, Biology, either Maths or Physics with at least a B in English	
Rest of UK Students: AAB at A-Level, including an A in Biology and Chemistry and a B in another subject	
At least one week of work experience in a Vet Clinic	
Four or more weeks of Animal Husbandry work experience - the broader the better	
Complete three supporting questionnaires that are emailed to you after the initial UCAS application	
Interview	

Royal Veterinary Collage - Five Years

RVC, located in London, constantly ranks as one of the best vet schools in the world. The gorgeous modern campus pulls in students from all over the globe. The course is accredited in countries everywhere. The interviews are in a MMI format, but there is also an observed group task - sounds pretty scary but I can assure it's actually a lot of fun. For every space on the course there are 5 applicants.

Required Tasks	Tick when complete
Scottish Students: at least BBB at National 5 in Physics, English and Maths	
Scottish Students: AAAAB at Higher including Chemistry and Biology	
Scottish Students: AA at Advanced Higher in Biology and Chemistry	
Rest of UK Students: AAAAAAA at GCSE including combined science or Chemistry and Biology, a B is required at English, Maths and Physics	
Rest of UK Students: AAA at A-Level in Chemistry, Biology and another subject	
70 Hours of work experience in one or most Vet Clinics	
70 Hours of Hands on Animal Husbandry work experience	
Complete the supplementary form (on the RVS website) BEFORE the UCAS deadline	
Interview	

Surrey - Five Years

Surrey was the newest vet school when I applied, it wasn't accredited yet, it still isn't as I write this, but I will be very shortly as the first cohort of students are going to graduate in the coming months. They once again have the newest facilities out there and the students absolutely love it there.

Required Tasks	Tick when complete
Scottish Students: AAABB at Higher, including As in Chemistry and Biology	
Scottish Students: AA at Advanced Higher in Chemistry and Biology	
Rest of UK Students: AAAAA at GCSE including Chemistry, Biology and Physics, at least a B in Maths and English	
Rest of UK Students: AAB at A-Level in Chemistry and Biology and another Subject	
Four weeks of animal related work experience, one must be in a Vet Clinic	
Complete the questionnaire form after the initial UCAS application	
Interview	

So, what vet schools are applying to? You still don't know? I suggest you make a pros and cons list for each university that you're considering. Here's one I made earlier. Go on, get writing.

Vet School	Pros	Cons

Personal Statement

The personal statement, those dreaded words still haunt me to this day. It's daunting, I know. I'd only complete this section if you're applying to vet school in the next few months, a lot can change in that time, and you want to put the best stuff you can in it. You have to amaze the admissions team. However, don't be too frightened by this, two of the vet schools I applied to don't even read your personal statement - I'm sure others won't either. This is your first opportunity to wow the vet school. Have your teachers look over it, your parents, even your friends. They need to be as critical as they can, you don't want to be sending a crappy personal statement off to the vet schools because people were too nice to you about it.

There are so many dos and don'ts in your personal statement, I'll try and break it down for you.

Do:
Talk about your work experience

Go in depth about a few placements you've done - talk about a wide variety of placements

Take a paragraph to explain what made you want to be a vet

Have a tiny paragraph (Im talking two or three lines) about your extracurriculars or job

Have a little bit of humour

Show your personality

In each paragraph refer back to how an experience will make you a great vet

Write it yourself - it has to sound like you

Let your passion shine through

Don't:
Use cliches (for example "ever since the day I was born I wanted to be a vet" - just no)

Use a thesaurus on every word - it makes you sound fake

Mention any specific vet schools - it will only make the others automatically want to reject you

Talk about your extracurriculars too much - they don't care if you're an avid gamer

List every placement you've done, if you don't go into detail, they don't care

But the best piece of advice I can give you is to just start it. Do it, right now, get your pencils out again. I want you to list your three most valuable - and diverse - work experience placements and list a reason why. For example, mine would be: Dairy Farm, I got to see the inside workings of a farm, I saw that the farmers cared more about their livestock than profit, unlike how the media portrays it. See, simple. Your turn.

●

●

●

Okay, now that you've done that, I want you to fill in the spaces below, this is a pretty general personal statement layout. In sentences, or in bullet points write as much as you can - it will help you in the long run if you do it now.

Why you want to be a Vet - No Cliches Remember

Work Experience 1 - What skills did you learn

Work Experience 2 - How did this impact your love for Veterinary

Work Experience 3 - Vet Med is very people based, maybe talk about that

Something Science related you've done, such as a science award you've won

Something else you've done that have given you the skills to become a good vet student - such as a job

The future - don't be too specific - but clarify what you hope to happen in the next 10 years in a sentence or two

And that's it, you have the basis of your personal statement, now get on your damn computer and get typing. Remember, you can only have 4000 characters in your personal statement, for me, it was almost a page of a Word document in size 11 writing. Okay what did I say? Get writing right now! Get that application in early for your own sanity. You'll thank me later.

The Wait

So, you've applied, yippee! But that's only the first battle, the second, is the wait. It's agonising for sure. Apart from questionnaires, I heard nothing from the vet schools at all for a month and a half. My friend on the other hand, got an unconditional, 24 hours after bloody applying. I checked my email everyday, I had nothing. You have to remember, you have school to be getting back to. I made excuses after excuses that couldn't do any revision because my application was so stressful, I regretted it when my mock exams came along (I even failed the Physics mock - oops). So get revising. Oh, what am I saying, you won't revise because a book told you so. I've added some fun games for you to procrastinate to.

Draw a realistic picture of your favourite animal

Riddles

Who makes it, has no need of it.
Who buys it, has no use for it.
Who uses it can neither see nor feel it.
What is it?

Answer:

I'm tall when I'm young and I'm short when I'm old.
What am I?

Answer:

Paul's height is six feet, he's an assistant at a butcher's shop, and wears size 9 shoes. What does he weigh?

Answer:

What kind of room has no windows and doors?

Answer:

There was a green house. Inside the green house there was a white house. Inside the white house there was a red house. Inside the red house there were lots of babies. What is it?

Answer:

Word search time!

Ocean Animal Word Search

```
S  L  S  E  Y  S  S  S  X  V  Z  E  E  C  Q
M  E  B  U  Q  N  T  H  J  H  S  N  R  Z  R
C  E  E  U  P  I  S  A  Y  A  E  O  N  J  S
S  S  I  R  N  O  B  R  L  I  S  M  N  R  T
J  D  E  G  O  Z  T  K  J  C  Y  E  L  I  A
G  E  R  M  A  L  C  C  Y  T  B  N  B  D  R
M  A  L  N  I  H  P  L  O  D  X  A  E  R  F
Y  V  S  L  O  B  S  T  E  R  T  E  R  T  I
X  U  D  B  Y  Y  C  F  E  Y  W  G  M  C  S
P  W  F  Z  Y  F  J  N  L  A  O  U  U  P  H
U  N  H  Q  W  L  I  B  E  R  H  B  B  M  L
Y  L  J  A  D  E  F  S  Z  Y  F  Y  I  G  F
J  F  M  G  L  C  L  M  H  F  V  Z  F  K  M
P  T  W  B  J  E  N  T  D  B  Q  X  H  A  T
S  W  O  R  D  F  I  S  H  U  D  C  W  Q  C
```

ANEMONE	**CLAM**	**CRAB**
DOLPHIN	**EEL**	**JELLYFISH**
LOBSTER	**OCTOPUS**	**SEAWEED**
SHARK	**SQUID**	**STARFISH**
STINGRAY	**SWORDFISH**	**WHALE**

Other things to do

- Search up 'The Periodic Table Song' on youtube and learn it - its not impossible I swear

- If you're up for a challenge, learn The Elements Song

- If you're feeling lazy, get on Netflix and watch your favourite show, relax that brain of yours

- Redecorate you room

- Make a homemade pizza, if that fails, order one from your favourite pizzeria

- If you have on, take your dog for a walk, teach them some new tricks!

Interviews

Interviews come around quicker than you think - in the span of a week, I went from hearing nothing to having three interviews! Thankfully Bristol don't interview so I didn't have to worry about them. Straight away I thought "What should I wear", now don't make the same mistake I did. I wore four inch black boots, while I looked stylish as hell, I fell down the stairs as I left an interview, another applicant caught me. How embarrassing could I be. Other than that, I think my burgundy blouse and black cigarette trousers did the trick. For men, I saw many with full on suits, and others with a casual coloured shirt and smart trousers. In all honesty, I don't think the interviewer care at all about what you wear - if you're decent, you'll be fine. BUT, you have to feel comfortable in what you wear, interviews can be pretty scary, you don't want your choice of clothing to make you feel even more self conscious, or un-comfy. You have be able to walk into that room like you are ready for anything they'll throw at you. You know what, draw yourself in your outfit below, see how damn good you look ;).

The best advice I was given for interview was to NOT fidget. A few years prior I lost the opportunity at a job because I could not stop fidgeting, it really distracts the interviewer and makes you look uncertain. You also want to have an open body position, no arm crossing, no constantly crossing and uncrossing your legs and most importantly, don't look at the floor the whole time. Imagine the interviewer is your friend, emphasis what you're talking about with subtle hand movements - but not too much. Look at them in the eye, smile when you talk about something you're super interested in. You might even find yourself enjoying it. They know you're nervous, but they're all super nice! Remember to introduce yourself with a handshake while making eye contact. Just keep smiling!!! (You know, unless you're talk about the ethics of euthanasia or something).

Now, you have to put in some effort before your interview date. You almost have to study for them. Research current ethical issues, and news stories. From memory, I could still tell you about the ethics and problems of badger culling and horse racing. I also studied how stem cell research happens, how dolly the sheep was made and many other things. I was 'lucky' enough that an outbreak of Mad Cow Disease had just occurred at a farm near me, this came up in my interview, and I was prepared, you should've seen how proud the interview was when I talked to him about it.

I can't give you specifics about the interviews - that would be unfair. Instead I'll give you a few quick tips that I was told about before mine. Know your cat and dog vaccines (I had to list them in two of my interviews), know your personal statement inside out and know what the hell you're talking about. When I tell my friends and family something from my work experience, I can emphasise stuff, and assume things as I go along. With your interviewer - you can't do this, they're most likely experts in the field and won't hesitate to correct you - believe me. Sometimes you can know about something in so much detail, that you forget to study the big picture - I'd forgotten what they remove in a spay for crying out loud.

Now for your turn. Pick 5 major ethical issues and write I paragraph on each one, make sure you know it, even bring this book to your interview and read it before you go in to refresh your memory. Here's my example:

Seaworld - There are many pros and cons. One the one hand, the money generated by tourists is used towards conservation efforts and research into the magical creatures they hold. By captivating some animals, they can maintain genetic diversity, educate the public, provide healthcare to sick marine life. They are protected from hunting and pollution and the people who care for them are in it because they love sea life. But at what cost does this come at. By entrapping the gorgeous creatures, they provide them with a life that lacks socialisation, they don't have enough space and they don't get enough activity. It has been found that these animals have a decreased lifespan, they can never be released once raised in a cage as they have no survival skills, they never learned how to hunt in their artificial environment.

Okay, your turn. Turn the page and start writing.

Remember, you have to talk about each side of the argument.

-

-

-

Good, now you've done that, you should be able to say something in the interview when asked about ethics or animal welfare, even if it's not about one of those issues, you should be able to figure it out.

Now, your personal statement, you need to know it. I walked into my interview and they had my personal statement laid out in front of them. They only asked me one question about it: "Tell me everything you know about Stem Cell Research" I word vomited everything I knew - I hope they were impressed. I only had one sentence on stem cell research in my personal statement and they chose it, so make sure you know everything about your statement. I personally spaced out every line of my personal statement and wrote a wee paragraph on each sentence. I recommend you do this in your own time.

Anyway, GOOD LUCK!!!!! It will be over before you know it and you may even get a few days off school for it yay! Do your best and don't keep thinking about everything that went wrong, I can assure you, most of it will go well without you even knowing it.

Handling Rejection

The majority of applicants go through it - rejection. I too was rejected by one of my choices. Luckily for me I already had two offers from my favourite schools so it didn't sting too bad. But I have to tell you, seeing someones face when they get rejected by all 4 schools is heartbreaking. It doesn't mean they won't be a good vet, it just means that they didn't have what the specific vet schools were looking for, another vet school will probably snatch them up the next year because they fit the applicant profile perfectly. If you've been rejected, please, don't let it get to you too much. Now you just have to make your application that bit stronger. If you haven't done your final exams yet, push to get the top grades, in your year out of school, get a job, gain some life experience. And importantly, get more work experience. It will hurt for now, but by the time you're finally accepted, you'll have more money, better skills and more life experience. A gap year can do so much for you, and you'll be so grateful for it in the long run. REMEMBER, rejection is just redirection in disguise. You *will* find your path to success.

You know what, I'll leave a blank page at the back of this book, if you want, write down the names of the vet schools that rejected you, or even just something random that's bothering you. Tear out the page, and rip it into tiny pieces. Chuck it in the (recycling) bin, and stop stressing yourself out about it, it helped me, maybe it will help you.

Persistance

You have to be persistent in this business. If you get rejected one year, try and try again, the vet schools admire students who reapply. Some schools ever favour it because it shows that you have the drive for the course. But if you got a place this year, WOW I'm so damn proud of you. You did it. Now you have a tough few years ahead of you. If you didn't get a place, I'm super proud of you as well, applying to vet school is a challenge, I'll be even prouder of you if you reapply again next year though, show those vet schools who's boss! I know you can do it. I've met people at open days applying for the forth time, and they went and bloody got a place. If it's the career for you, you'll do it.

Thank You

Thank you so much for pushing to the end of my wee book. I hope you enjoyed. By the way *SPOILERS* the answers to those riddles were: a coffin, a candle, meat, mushrooms, and a watermelon. HOPE YOU ENJOYED! I wish you the best of luck in the future!

This is the page for you to rip out. Enjoy.

Printed in Poland
by Amazon Fulfillment
Poland Sp. z o.o., Wrocław

51333941R00027